THE KIDS WI

MW01037254

Empowering Young Minds through the Law of Attraction

Shantelee R. Brown

Empowering Young Minds through the Law of Attraction

Dedication

To my unconceived children Theo'mar and Zamarla who are the main and only character in this book; as well as my nieces and nephew Alliandra, Chelsea-Ann and CJ; and to my beautiful cousins Rushaleigh and Chris-Ali Kavanaugh. I dedicate this book to all of you because you guys deserve to have a much better life than I did. I know this book will serve you all very well.

With love from your favorite aunt and cousin

~Shantelee R. Brown

THE KIDS WHO KNOW MORE

Empowering Young Minds through the Law of Attraction

Shantelee R. Brown

Contents

About the Author

My name is Shantelee Brown; I enjoy learning new things, writing, traveling, being in nature, and cooking among a host of other things.

I was born on September 9th, 1989 at the Princess Margaret Hospital in Saint Thomas, Jamaica, West Indies, and raised in the most beautiful parish on the island -Portland.

I later migrated to the United States of America and lived in New York City for ten years before moving to sunny San Diego, California. While in New York City, I studied psychology at the City University of New York (CUNY).

It was during my time at CUNY that I had discovered how good I am at expressing myself through written words, after being complimented on my writing skills by numerous professors.

I began writing poems and later published my first book, titled "The Shadow Side of An Introvert" (not for kids) in December of 2017.

I started following new age teachings back in the summer of 2012 and was later introduced to an awesome book called "The Secret" by a distant relative.

The book has helped me in tremendous ways to contextualize what I've been taught growing up in the church as a child. I have come to realize that faith and prayers really work in the same ways the law of attraction and affirmations does. Understanding this has given me a great deal of confidence in my ability to create the life that I knew innately that I was born to live.

Now, I speak things into existence rather than praying and wondering if anyone out there in the great unknown will hear and answer me.

Introduction

It is my hope that this book will be a guiding light and the

gift of wisdom that I never had at a very young age.

I wrote this book in hope of inspiring young boys and girls

to challenge themselves; to dream big and to work even

harder to ensure that their big dreams will transform lives and

turn out to be multi-million-dollar sources of income at a

young age.

It is my humble opinion that information is grasped easier at

a young age… I still struggle from time to time to stay on a

positive path, even with the wealth of information that I

have on the subject of the law of attraction.

I have to be constantly dragging myself back on track;

luckily for me I am aware when I am drifting away from the

things that I want to attract into my life and can easily realign

myself to be a match to the thing I desire. I say that to say

this, if I had known about the law of attraction from,

I was a child or even as teenager I would find it much easier to apply it to my daily life. Let me be clear, applying the law of attraction isn't the problem; the problem is in getting rid of years of negative conditionings.

The Discovery

Once upon a time, there was a little boy and a little girl named Theo'mar and Zamarla who believed that they could achieve anything they set their minds to, and so they did.

They also discovered the power of using positive affirmations and vision boards to keep them motivated and to work continuously at achieving the goals that they have set for themselves.

They have also come to realized that expressing gratitude is not only a nice thing to do but can serve as a powerful tool in the manifestation process as well.

Each year on the first of January they would joyfully create a new vision board to reflect their desires for that year.

They would decorate the vision board with pictures and notes. Notes stating why a particular goal is important for them and what emotions they would feel when the goals are achieved.

Here is an example of a vision board

Positive Affirmations for Children

One Sunday evening Zamarla, and Theo'mar, went for a walk in the park and as they walked along the lake in silence, Zamarla said to Theo'mar, this is a very nice place; we should sit here by the lake and start writing our affirmations now! And so, they did. I am happy and grateful now that I have made the Honor Roll at school, said Zamarla; she looked over at theo'mar, he smiles and said,

I am happy and grateful to have been born in a home filled with love and laughter. They both laughed and said we should just come together and compiled a list of positive affirmations so that other little boys and girls can benefit from.

And so, they spent the rest of their evening in the park at the lake side writing positive affirmations.

I am healthy and strong.

I am loved.

I am smart.

I am a great communicator.

I am financially well off at a young age.

I make my parents proud by getting excellent grades in

school.

I am very good at playing sports.

I am a magnet that attracts only good things.

I am extremely good at managing my time and the resources

I get from my parents.

I have very supportive parents.

I am a future world leader.

I am a successful business owner.

I am a master at saving money.

I am kind to my peers.

I am an upstanding citizen; my morals and values are of good

standing.

I am creative.

I am in harmony with the universe.

The universe is working overtime to fulfill all my heart's desires.

I am apart of God.

I am very successful in everything I do.

I am accepted into the University of my Choice and I graduate with honors.

Wherever I go I make others feel happy and loved.

I am a light in any dark situation that I may encounter in life.

I am blessed beyond my years.

I am a very intuitive person.

I am an understanding person and I am therefore understood.

I am wise.

I value myself, and so does everyone else around me.

I am prosperous.

People love and accept me for who I am.

I deserve all the love, support and abundance that are present in my life.

Everything I need will appear in my life at the perfect time.

Happiness is my birthright.

By allowing myself to be happy I inspire others to be happy as well.

My heart is overflowing with joy.

I find solutions to challenges and roadblocks easily and move past them very quickly.

Mistakes and setbacks are steppingstones that lead to my success because I learn from them quickly.

I love change and easily adjust myself to new situations.

Self-confidence is what I thrive on; nothing is impossible, and life is great.

My home is a peaceful sanctuary where I feel safe and happy.

Calmness washes over me with every deep breath I take.

I am free of anxiety, and a calm inner peace fills my mind and body.

I release the past and live fully in the present moment.

All is well in my world. I am calm, happy and content.

Empowering Young Minds through the Law of Attraction

Now that we are finished writing our affirmations and making our vision board what do you suggest we do? Ask Theo'mar.

I suggest that we share more of what we discovered about the Law of Attraction with every little boy and girl right across the length and breadth of the world, so they too can start unlocking a life filled with wonderful possibilities like we did, Zamarla replied.

The Law of Attraction Explained

In accordance with the Law of Attraction, you attract into your life things, circumstances and conditions that correspond with the nature of your dominant thoughts and beliefs, both consciously and subconsciously. Every area of your life, including your health, your finances, how well you perform in school and all your relationships, are influenced by this great Universal Law. The Law of Attraction is often referred to as "the Basic Law of the Universe" which states that: "like attracts like".

Everything, including yourself, your thoughts and anything else you may or may not want to experience, is pure energy vibrating at different frequencies. The basic premise of the Law of Attraction is that like energy attracts like energy. You attract to yourself that which you are in vibrational harmony with, not that which you long for or even deserve. Your dominant frequency is determined by your dominant mental attitude, which itself is determined by your habitual thoughts and beliefs. Simply put, a positive mental attitude attracts positive experiences and circumstances while a negative mental attitude attracts those conditions that we deem negative or unwanted.

To consciously attract anything, you want to experience into your life, you must need it, simply wanting something isn't enough, to make you a vibrational match. You must have a purpose for it and when something has a big enough purpose; it becomes a necessity rather than a luxury.

You are able to attract anything you need to yourself because you are already connected to everything, seen and unseen. Nothing and no one is separate from you. The sense of separation we experience in the physical world is created by the way our five senses interpret this infinite sea of vibrating energy. You are one with the One Universal Mind from which all things become manifest. The creative power of your thoughts is limitless within the realm of that which is possible.

Empowering Young Minds through the Law of Attraction

You must learn to bring the energy of your thoughts and your actions into vibrational harmony with the things you need, be it perfect health, success, abundance, long-lasting friendship, excellent grades, getting accepted into the college or anything else.

Creative visualization is the basic technique by which you can positively and effectively reprogram your subconscious mind and begin to attract to yourself those things and circumstances that you consciously choose.

Don't Play the Blame Game: Understanding the Law of Attraction is not about blaming yourself or anyone else for the negative or unwanted conditions in your life. Getting caught up in this blame game would only serve to attract more of those things that you do not want. This knowledge is intended to empower you to take full responsibility for your current conditions by understanding the attraction power of your thoughts.

Know that by taking responsibility for your life, you also grant yourself the power to change it.

Matchmaker, Matchmaker Bring Me My Match: The bottom line is that you attract to yourself that which you think about a lot. There is no judgment call involved about whether a particular thought is "good" or "bad" or whether its corresponding circumstance is "deserved" or "underserved". The Law of Attraction is neutral. It does not judge, punish or reward. It simply serves to bring like energy together. Think of it as the great matchmaker. You set your standard via your habitual thoughts and beliefs and it brings you your perfect vibratory match, every time.

You do not have to learn to work with or apply the Law of Attraction. Being a Universal Law, it is already working perfectly in your life, whether or not you understand or accept it, and it never ceases to operate. Your primary goal is to adjust your mental attitude by changing your predominant thoughts and beliefs while creating a need or purpose for that which you want to create in your life. To become the master of your life, you must master your mind (always think happy uplifting and positive thoughts), not the Law of Attraction. It is already a master unto itself.

The Law of Attraction is the basic Universal Law which holds everything together but there are eleven more Universal Laws, (I will quickly list them here but will not go into detail about them –The Law of Divine Oneness, The Law of Vibration,

The Law of Cause and effect, The Law of Action, The Law of Correspondence, The Law of Compensation, The Law of Perpetual Transmutation of Energy, The Law of Relativity, The Law of Polarity, The Law of Rhythm and The Law of Gender).

By understanding all the Laws of the Universe, you will be able to understand the true nature of reality and how you can have the life you have always wanted. To experience profound transformation in any area of your life, you must first become conscious of the truth that the circumstances of

your outside world correspond precisely with the nature of

your inner world and are attracted to you by the Law of

Attraction.

According to this Universal Law, like energy attracts like

energy. Whether you understand it or not it is still at work in

your life; it is in your best interest to understand and use it to

your advantage.

To attract the things, you desire into your life you must learn

to bring your thoughts and your actions into vibrational

harmony with the essence of your choice and leave the rest

up to the Law of Attraction. Essentially, all you need to do is

work on yourself.

Inspiring Quotes

"You cannot fail while you are still trying." ~Shantelee

Brown

"Everything you can imagine is real."

~Pablo Picasso

Promise Yourself:

"To be so strong that nothing

Can disturb your peace of mind.

To talk health, happiness, and prosperity

to every person you meet.

To make all your friends feel

that there is something in them

To look at the sunny side of everything

and make your optimism come true.

To think only the best, to work only for the best,

and to expect only the best.

To be just as enthusiastic about the success of others

Empowering Young Minds through the Law of Attraction

as you are about your own.

To forget the mistakes of the past

and press on to the greater achievements of the future.

To wear a cheerful countenance at all times

and give every living creature you meet a smile.

To give so much time to the improvement of yourself

that you have no time to criticize others.

To be too large for worry, too noble for anger, too strong for

fear, and too happy to permit the presence of trouble.

To think well of yourself and to proclaim this fact to the

world,

not in loud words but great deeds.

To live in faith that the whole world is on your side

so long as you are true to the best that is in you."

~Christian D. Larson

"All judgments of ourselves are first conceived within our own minds... then we go about our daily lives consciously or unconsciously looking for confirmation." ~Shantelee Brown.

"Do not go where the path may lead, go instead where there is no path and leave a trail."

~Ralph Waldo Emerson

"No one can make you feel inferior without your consent"

~Eleanor Roosevelt

"Do one thing every day that scares you." ~Eleanor Roosevelt

"You have power over your mind not outside events. Realize this, and you will find strength. ~Marcus Aurelius

"If you want to be happy, do not dwell in the past, do not worry about the future, focus on living fully in the present."

~Roy .T. Bennett

"Don't be pushed around by the fear in your mind. Be led by the dreams in your heart. ~Roy T. Bennett

"Make improvements, not excuses. Seek respect, not attention." ~Roy T. Bennett

"Be brave to stand for what you believe in even if you stand alone." ~Roy T. Bennett

"Surround yourself with people who believe in your dreams and avoid people who tell you that you can't." ~Shantelee R. Brown

"Winning doesn't always mean being first. Winning means you're doing better than you've done before." ~Bonnie Blair

"Positive thinking will let you do everything better than negative thinking will." ~Zig Ziglar

"Every day may not be good…but there's something good in every day." ~Alice Morse Earle

"Be so happy that, when other people look at you, they become happy too." ~Anonymous

The Power of Expressing Gratitude

An attitude of gratitude can help you in all areas of your life! When you are grateful you feel happier and less envious of others and what they have. You become more optimistic about life and your self-esteem increase. An attitude of gratitude can even boost your health...ungrateful people stress a lot about what they don't have; many studies have shown that stress is the driving force behind a lot of sickness in our society today. People who are grateful tend to have more friends, because the truth is, nobody wants to be around people who are unhappy and complaining all the time.

1. **Gratitude makes us happier.**

By taking as little as five minutes out of your day each day to journal thing that you are grateful for can increase your well-being by more than ten percent according to research.

2. Gratitude makes people like us.

Empowering Young Minds through the Law of Attraction

Gratitude makes us nicer, more trusting, more social, and more appreciative. As a result, it helps us make more friends, deepen our existing relationships.

 or

Who are you? Ungrateful Joe in the dark by yourself or popular Tom in the light with his friends?

3. Gratitude makes us healthier.

Gratitude can strengthen your physiological functioning and improves positive emotions. Many people who make it a habit to keep a gratitude journal have reported positive changes to

their immune system, faster recovery after an illness or

medical procedure and an overall feeling of improved health

and more energy throughout their day.

4. Gratitude strengthens our emotions.

Gratitude reduces feelings of envy, makes us happier, lets us

experience good feelings and helps us bounce back from

stress easily.

Below you'll see pictures of a grateful heart on the right and

an ungrateful heart to your left.

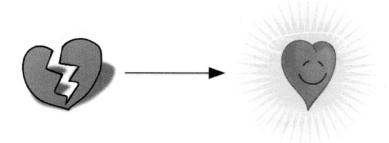

5. Gratitude makes us more optimistic.

Gratitude is strongly associated with optimism. Optimism, in turn, makes us happier, improves our health, and has been shown to increase lifespan by a few years.

6. Gratitude increases self-esteem.

A 2014 study published in the *Journal of Applied Sports Psychology* found that gratitude increased athletes' self-esteem, an essential component to optimal performance. Other studies have shown that gratitude reduces social comparisons.

Rather than becoming resentful toward people who have more money or better jobs—a major factor in reduced self-esteem; grateful people are able to appreciate other people's accomplishments and be motivated by it rather than becoming jealous.

7. Gratitude helps us bounce back.

Those who are more grateful have a more proactive coping style and are more likely to have and seek out social support in times of needs and are less likely to develop depression and are more likely to grow in times of difficulties rather than to be stressed.

8. Gratitude Aides in the Manifestation Process.

Gratitude is a powerful Law of Attraction exercise. It raises your vibration and brings you into harmony with the energy of the universe.

Gratitude is no cure-all, but it is a massively underutilized tool for improving health, happiness, abundance and life's-satisfaction.

Reassurance for Young Minds

Hello, young minds! Today is the day that you will unlock the awesome potentials within you. Today you will learn the tools necessary to be tomorrow's leaders. Understand that you are wonderfully and powerfully made. Understand that God wants you to be creative innovators. He wants you to be successful in your finances, in your education, in your love life when that time comes. He wants you to be healthy and strong emotionally, physically and spiritually.

It's okay to let your mind wander. It's okay to dream big. In fact, every dream you have should be enormous.

The greatest thing you can ever do for yourself -is to believe in yourself.

A Poem from the Author to you!

Beautiful Children

Beautiful children that is what you are.

Hold up your head and reach for the stars.

I sing praises on your behalf, for a future well bright and

filled with sparks.

Beautiful children take pride in yourselves and don't let

anyone make you feel less than you are.

Beautiful children you can have a piece of my heart, so don't

go into hiding when your families and friends break your

heart.

Just continue to say, 'I am a beautiful child, and I will reach

for the stars because the future depends on what's in my

heart.'

-Always remember that I love you and I am cheering for

you. You will succeed!

Empowering Young Minds through the Law of Attraction

WORKSHEET

On the next few pages I have created a template for you to start your very own affirmation and gratitude journals as well as a space for you to set short- and long-term goals.

Ask yourself these questions:

Who am I? Am I happy with the person that I am today? Who do I want to become? What am I most grateful for in life? What will it take for me to become the person I want to be? How do I get to that place where I am the best version of myself?

Once you've answered the questions above it will become easier for you to complete the 14-day worksheets.

AFFIRMATION JOURNAL

Now, it's time for you to create your very own affirmation journal; remember to always write your affirmations in the present-tense or begin with the words, "I AM".

Day 1.

Affirmation Journal

Day 2.

Affirmation Journal

Day 3.

Affirmation Journal

Day 4.

Affirmation Journal

Day 5.

Empowering Young Minds through the Law of Attraction

Affirmation Journal

Day 6.

Affirmation Journal

Day 7.

Affirmation Journal

Day 8.

Empowering Young Minds through the Law of Attraction

Affirmation Journal

Day 9.

Affirmation Journal

Day 10.

Empowering Young Minds through the Law of Attraction

Affirmation Journal

Day 11.

Affirmation Journal

Day 12.

Affirmation Journal

Day 13.

Affirmation Journal

Day 14.

Gratitude Journal

Day 1. What are you most grateful for?

Empowering Young Minds through the Law of Attraction

Gratitude Journal

Day 2. What are you most grateful for?

Gratitude Journal

Day 3. What are you most grateful for?

Gratitude Journal

Day 4. What are you most grateful for?

Empowering Young Minds through the Law of Attraction

Gratitude Journal

Day 5. What are you most grateful for?

Gratitude Journal

Day 6. What are you most grateful for?

Gratitude Journal

Day 7. What are you most grateful for?

Gratitude Journal

Day 8. What are you most grateful for?

Gratitude Journal

Day 9. What are you most grateful for?

Gratitude Journal

Day 10. What are you most grateful for?

Gratitude Journal

Day 11. What are you most grateful for?

Gratitude Journal

Day 12. What are you most grateful for?

Gratitude Journal

Day 13. What are you most grateful for?

Gratitude Journal

Day 14. What are you most grateful for?

Empowering Young Minds through the Law of Attraction

Goal Setting

When setting goals, you should start with your long-term goals then create smaller goals that will help you to achieve your long-term goals. Write down what action is needed for your goals to become a reality and work towards them.

A short-term goal is one that you can achieve within 3-12 months and a long-term goal will take anywhere from 1-5 years.

What would you do if you knew you couldn't fail?

Long-term goals	Short-term goals	Action Steps

Goal Setting

What would you do if you knew you couldn't fail?

Long-term goals	Short-term goals	Action Steps

Goal Setting

What would you do if you knew you couldn't fail?

Long-term goals	Short-term goals	Action Steps

Empowering Young Minds through the Law of Attraction

Thank You Note!

Thank you for your purchasing my book…

It is my hope that this book will inspire you to aspire towards goals that will make others call you crazy for even considering them but will later try to emulate you for achieving what was once thought of as a crazy idea.

If you enjoyed reading this book, please go to amazon.com/author/shanteleebrown and give it a five-star rating and let me know in the comment section how you benefit from reading this book. By reviewing this book, you will help to make it more visible to other readers.

Again, a grateful heat says, thank you!

Made in the USA
Middletown, DE
04 August 2022

70521469R00040